Colorado National Monument ignited its 100th anniversary celebration with a first-ever fireworks display in the park on New Year's Eve, 2010. ■ *Photo by Jeff Kochevar*

Monumental Majesty

100 years of Colorado National Monument

THE DAILY SENTINEL
GJSentinel.com

Edited by Laurena Mayne Davis
Cover and interior design by Robert García
ISBN 978-0-578-07496-2

■ *Cover, inside cover, inside back cover and title page photos by Christopher Tomlinson*

The Daily Sentinel saved the following resources by using responsible paper choices. These papers were made in the USA, are FSC® certified, are made with 10% recycled fiber and were processed chlorine free.

 Preserved 6 trees for the future

 Saved 2,687 gallons of wastewater flow

 Conserved 4,480,945 BTUs of energy

 Did not generate 297 pounds of solid waste

 Prevented 585 pounds of greenhouse gases

 Did not create 18 pounds of water-borne waste

MIX
Paper from responsible sources
FSC® C023568

■ *Photo by Christopher Tomlinson*

CONTENTS

Foreword   V

Introduction   VII

Chapter 1: Founders and Builders

Monument Natives   1
Tireless Trailblazer   4
Walter Walker and Sentinel Support   10
Otto's Best Friend   14
Homesteaders and John Otto   16
New Deal at Work   18

Chapter 2: Natural World

Classic Rock: Best of the Stones   33
Ancient Life   36
The Bone Hunter   39
Desert in Bloom   42
All Creatures Great and Small   50
A Rare Find   57
Where the Buffalo Roamed   58

Chapter 3: Grand Valley's Backyard

Monument Within a Monument   63
On the Trail   67
Run to Glory   70
Riding the Rim   72
What's in a Name?   77
With This Ring ...   78
Otto Meets His Match   80
The Long and Winding Road   82

Chapter 4: Art and Culture

The Monument as Canvas   90
Picture This   106
       Tomlinson   107
       Daugherty   113
       Humphrey   115
       Kurtzman   117
       Traudt   120
Star of the Show   124

Thanks   126

Epilogue   127

Foreword

▪ *Photo by Cable Risdon*

" 'Monumental Majesty' is a stunning book, full of exquisite imagery of one of the most beautiful places on the planet. But it is also a superb history, a narrative about, among other things, the people who fought to set aside this place for us to enjoy forever."

— Ken Burns

Ken Burns has been making documentary films for more than 25 years and is the creator, director and producer of numerous award-winning documentaries including "Jazz," "The Civil War" and "Baseball." Burns' six-part series "The National Parks: America's Best Idea" honors both the dramatic landscapes and the people who devoted themselves to saving some precious portion of the land they loved for everyone to enjoy.

"Climb the mountains and get their good tidings, Nature's peace will flow into you as sunshine flows into trees. The winds will blow their own freshness into you and the storms their energy, while cares will drop off like autumn leaves." — John Muir, "Our National Parks," 1901

■ *Photo by Ann Driggers*

Introduction

By Jay Seaton, Grand Junction Daily Sentinel publisher

■ *Photo by Ann Driggers*

It is folly, I think, to attempt to convey in words the stomach-quivering awe of your first trip over Colorado National Monument. Most people drive it, hands clenching the steering wheel on the winding ascent. As the terrain falls away beside the car, the views become increasingly lunar. And spectacular.

We have John Otto to thank for introducing us to the exotic wonders of what was once considered by white settlers nothing more than a series of dead-end canyons, good for little more than grazing (or hiding) livestock. Alone, Otto built trails through the area — some of which exist to this day — in an attempt to make the formidable terrain more accessible.

Otto achieved his dream of waking the world to the beauty and power of what is now Colorado National Monument. This book aims to add some color and flavor to the 100-year anniversary of that achievement.

Otto probably did not realize that Colorado National Monument would become one of the most accessible land treasures in the world. Its proximity to a metropolitan area makes it unique. People living in the Grand Valley refer to it as "our backyard" and "our playground," though its 100 years as a national monument have endeared it to millions around the world.

The Grand Junction Daily Sentinel, situated within view of the monument, has chronicled in pictures and words the monument's birth and close relationship to its community. Indeed, Sentinel Publisher Walter Walker's support of Otto's efforts gave a foothold to what may otherwise have been interpreted as the tinkerings of a madman on a mountain.

We hope the following pages allow you to visit, or revisit memories of, our backyard national park. Better yet, we hope this book inspires you to seize the opportunity Otto afforded us by, in Walker's words, "opening this lovely wilderness to man's footsteps."

Whether you enjoy running its trails, pedaling over its summit, exploring its desert wildlife or white-knuckling it over historic Rim Rock Drive, Colorado National Monument is bountiful with good tidings.

Get them.

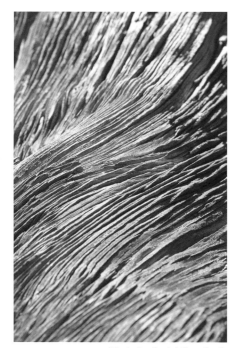

■ *Photo by Gretel Daugherty*

Jay Seaton gets a jolt every morning when he opens the bedroom shades and finds beyond his backyard that — whoa! what is that? — Independence Monument stands in the distance.

Morning fog dissipates enough to reveal Balanced Rock, estimated at 600 tons, on its precarious perch. ■ *Photo by Christopher Tomlinson*

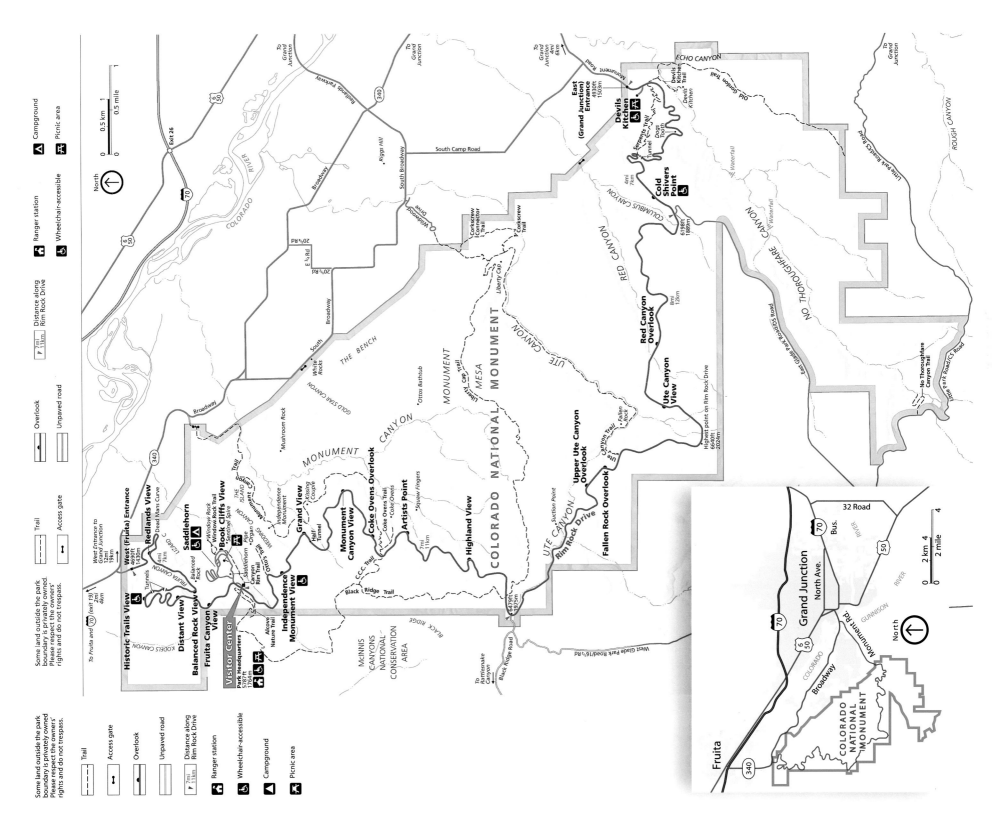

The Utes visited what is now Colorado National Monument from at least the late 1300s until 1881. These petroglyphs — pictures etched into rock — were made by the Utes. Park Ranger Briana Board explains the proper etiquette to use when visiting one of these fragile and non-renewable cultural resources. Visitors should never touch a rock art panel as oils in the hand can erode petroglyphs and destroy the patina. Visitors should stick to trails and not introduce any foreign substance to attempt to enhance the images. ■ *Photo by Christopher Tomlinson*

Chapter 1: Founders and Builders

Monument Natives

By Bob Silbernagel

John Otto became infatuated with what is now known as Colorado National Monument early in the 20th century.

But he was a latecomer.

The 1877 Hayden Survey maps of Colorado show No Thoroughfare Canyon, within what is now the monument, evidence that white people had been visiting and naming the area even before the region was open to settlement.

For thousands of years prior to that, early Americans crisscrossed what is now western Colorado. Some left reminders of their visits to the red sandstone canyons — rock drawings, pieces of pottery, arrowheads.

Evidence of American Indian visitors to the monument has been found dating from the Paleo-Indian era, which extends back nearly 10,000 years. Those visitors are believed to be members of the Clovis culture, with origins in central Asia.

The people we call the Anasazi, or Ancestral Puebloans — famous for their cliff dwellings of the Four Corners region — didn't frequent the monument. It would have been at the extreme northern boundary of their territory.

However, the Fremont people, who inhabited much of this region until about 1300, are believed to have visited and left relics of their visits in the rocks of the monument.

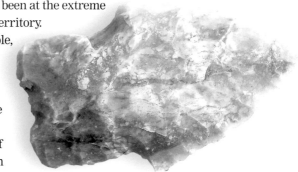

Lithic point ■ *Photo by Christopher Tomlinson*

But the greatest evidence of American Indian visitation in the monument is by the Utes, who made western Colorado their home from at least the late 1300s until most of them were forced from Colorado to Utah in 1881.

Within the boundaries of the monument are a number of sites believed to have Ute origins — petroglyphs and pictographs, remnants of wikiups, and fallen tree platforms that may have once been temporary burial sites.

Although it's difficult to interpret the meaning of individual drawings, Ute leaders believe there is a sanctity to the monument's rock spires and deep canyons that might well have drawn their ancestors seeking a place to pray and connect with the natural and spiritual world.

Some of the Utes' thoughts are recorded in "Talking About a Sacredness: An Ethnographic Overview of Colorado National Monument" by Sally McBeth, a cultural anthropologist from the University of Northern Colorado.

Monument officials will continue to promote the protection and conservation of archaelogical sites through monitoring, archives, research and public education.

While 21st century visitors to the monument continue to be awestruck by its beauty and geologic wonders, we would do well to remember and honor those who came here long ago.

Bob Silbernagel is editorial page editor for The Daily Sentinel and enjoys hiking, biking and horseback riding in the spectacular lands of western Colorado.

Overleaf — Pinyon pines flank a contorted juniper on Colorado National Monument. Far off in the distance are the striated Bookcliffs, frosted white. The Bookcliffs range extends some 200 miles, east to west, from De Beque Canyon in Colorado to Price Canyon in Utah. ■ *Photo by Rob Kurtzman*

Willow basket ■ *Photo by Christopher Tomlinson*

Tireless Trailblazer

By Gary Harmon

Difficult as it might be to imagine, settlers who moved into the Grand Valley in the 1880s took little interest in the uplift to the south, where the precipitous cliffs, rocky spires and basalt bottom offered little in the way of their immediate needs for open lands that easily could be irrigated and harvested.

A rancher might tuck away some cattle and sheep in a box canyon, but the appreciation for the wonders of nature's powers of sculpting and carving pretty much ended there.

That was until a Missouri-born itinerant union organizer, tart critic of his detractors, patriot, purist, pioneer and, at least to some authorities, dangerously crazed man by the name of John Otto stumbled onto its secrets and declared it his mission to unveil to the world the sand and ochre canyons overlooking the Colorado River.

After arriving in western Colorado in approximately 1906, Otto went to work building trails, dubbed "monuments" the monoliths of hard rock left behind by the vagaries of erosion, and scaled the one he dubbed Independence Monument.

Working alone with but

John Otto's California grave marker. ■ *Photo by Christopher Tomlinson*

Daily Sentinel reporter Whipple Chester took this photo of John Otto, top, and Rae Kennedy pounding metal pipe into Independence Monument as hand and foot holds for climbing. ■ *Photo provided by National Park Service*

his dogs, donkeys, horse, shovels and picks for company, Otto built paths through the forbidding canyons, if "built" is indeed the word for digging, chiseling and rearranging loose rock and soil into paths and trails.

It was via those narrow walkways that Otto hoped to make possible the steep and winding climbs he had navigated into places he had given evocative titles, such as Monument Canyon and Jefferson Monument, with its smaller, adjacent monuments named for three "martyred" presidents: Lincoln, Garfield and McKinley.

Eager as Otto was to share with the world his wonderland of rusty-red and orange rim rocks, he was quick to battle those he perceived as enemies of the dream he saw culminated in 1911, when President William Howard Taft designated his 17,000-acre "Garden of Eden" a national monument, which later was expanded to more than 20,000 acres.

He was the first custodian of the monument, a job he held some 16 years.

Otto moved to California in about 1933, where he panned gold in the Klamath River until he died in Yreka in 1952.

He never returned to the territory known for its unpredictable landscape fraught with peril for the unwary, yet graceful and rewarding for those willing to approach with care the place where a man who saw things others ignored found his rough and rocky metaphor.

Gary Harmon, senior reporter for The Daily Sentinel, routinely stops what he's doing in Grand Junction to peer up Monument Canyon and marvel at the sunlit solitude of Independence Monument.

From this aerial vantage, Serpents Trail can be seen snaking to the right and Rim Rock Drive wending to the left. Serpents Trail was engineered by John Otto and was the primary access to Colorado National Monument before Rim Rock Drive was built. ■ *Photo by Christopher Tomlinson*

"One of his best known achievements was the Serpentine trail, or Trail of the Serpent, the old approach to Rim Rock Drive of Colorado National Monument," The Daily Sentinel wrote in a 1952 obituary for John Otto. "Mr. Otto laid out the tortuous, steep road many years ago and did much of the work on it. It served for many years as an access to Glade Park and Pinyon Mesa before the Rim Rock Drive was built. A new road up No Thoroughfare Canyon has replaced the Serpentine trail, frightening to easterners not used to the mountains, a thrill to daredevils riding by car, bicycle or motorcycle, but an everyday experience for livestockmen and their families who traveled it almost daily."

A hiker left behind a raised bootprint on Coke Ovens Trail. ■ *Photo by Christopher Tomlinson*

Opposite — Specialized trail builders with the National Park Service pick and leverage stone on a section of trail in Colorado National Monument in 2010. Although separated by a hundred years from fervent trail builder John Otto, the methods employed by contemporary trail builders are much the same. ■ *Photo by Christopher Tomlinson*

Tools of the trail builders' trade. ■ *Photo by Christopher Tomlinson*

A near full moon sets over Colorado National Monument. ■ *Photo by Christopher Tomlinson*

The monument is open year-round, with generally mild winter temperatures ranging from 20 to 45 degrees. Here, National Park Service employees clear snow from a scenic overlook by the visitor center. Spring daytime highs average in the mid-60s, while summer temperatures can climb to 100 degrees in the inner canyons. The wettest months are usually March and October. ■ *Photo by Christopher Tomlinson*

Walter Walker and Sentinel Support

By Charles Ashby

With Daily Sentinel headlines such as "Almost Sure to Get a Park," "Means Much to This City" and "Up to People to Boost Park," it's clear John Otto had a booster in his local newspaper.

Walter Walker

Walter Walker, in various editorial roles at the Sentinel over the years, either wrote or encouraged numerous articles about Otto's efforts, including a lengthy column about a tour he and other members of the Grand Junction Chamber of Commerce took in the spring of 1909. In it, he wrote:

"The drive from Grand Junction to what John Otto calls the Grand Junction entrance to the cañon is easy and pleasant and interesting. Down Fifth Street, across two rivers, through the rich lands of the Red Mesa, up the No Thoroughfare Cañon road for a time, then branching off to the west and south, and, after a drive of an hour and a half from Grand Junction, you reach the foot of the remarkable trail that has been built by John Otto."

In the ensuing two years, the Sentinel published numerous letters and news items about the monument and Otto's attempts to get federal designation for it. It led many others to take that same drive, which today takes about 15 minutes. When Otto came to town, he dropped by the newspaper's office to give Walker updates about the monument, which the editor

A Daily News photographer captured this John Otto-led tour of Grand Mesa. (The photographer's shadow is visible at the bottom.) Otto lobbied to have Grand Mesa and Colorado National Monument united into one Colorado National Park. ■ *Photo provided by National Park Service*

Even after John Otto had moved away, he continued to correspond with Walter Walker of The Daily Sentinel, as in this 1949 letter addressed to the publisher as "Mr. Old Timer." ■ *Photo by Christopher Tomlinson*

would put in the next day's paper.

Otto sent a copy of Walker's column to President William Taft, who later visited the city on Sept, 22, 1909.

In addition to a detailed account of what he saw on the monument, Walker wrote at length of Otto's dream to get federal status for what then was known as the Monument Cañons park:

"All the time he was endeavoring to arouse interest in the great playground and show ground of nature. Few people knew anything of the undeveloped section of which he talked. Few paid any heed to his statements and his plans. He was put down as a dreamer. Perhaps he is a dreamer, but his dreams have a wonderful degree of materiality and substance."

Charles Ashby, who has a spectacular view of Colorado National Monument from his patio, is the political reporter for The Daily Sentinel and a history buff.

Grand Junction Gets Land Set Apart For A Great National Park

On Jan. 1, 1910, The Daily Sentinel announced on Page One that the secretary of the Interior Department had cleared the way for a national park to be established.

Headlined "Grand Junction Gets Lands Set Apart For A Great National Park," the story reported, in part: "Grand Junction is to get the great national park she has so long wanted. The dream of John Otto, the trail builder and guardian spirit of the magnificent Monument Park country, is realized. The fight inaugurated and pushed by The Daily Sentinel, aided by a number of public-spirited local men, to get this true Garden of the Gods that is just without the gates of Grand Junction set aside as a national park has won out. ... The Daily Sentinel rejoices over the part it took in securing the Monument Canon National Park. For months and months it has urged the advisability of this action, or from the time that John Otto told his story of the marvelous beauty of that natural playground. The Sentinel has urged the matter while others, who had not investigated the possibilities of such a park, were lukewarm. It engaged the attention and loyal support of Senator Hughes and Congressman Taylor and these two men went right to Secretary Ballinger with the matter."

The new park was established on May 24, 1911, but word did not get out of Washington, D.C., right away, nor accurately. On May 25, 1911, the Sentinel cited a wire story as saying the name of the park would be Monolithic National Monument. For its part, that same day The Daily Sentinel ran its own story, claiming that John Otto and his fiancee were to be married atop Independence Monument, a supposed plan debunked by John Otto himself sometime later.

Overleaf – Independence Monument, just after sunrise. ■ *Photo by Christopher Tomlinson*

Otto's Best Friend

By Mike Wiggins

Young Daily Sentinel reporter Whipple Chester explored canyons with John Otto, stood as best man at his wedding and remained close to the monument's first custodian long after both left Colorado.

Chester photographed many of Otto's exploits. One is of the eccentric pioneer pounding metal pipes into the side of Independence Monument, making it easier to scale the monolith. Several show Otto sitting astride his horse, scouting trails.

"Whipple admired John. Out of all of the people in Grand Junction, Whipple Chester was probably John Otto's best friend," said author Alan Kania, whose biography on Otto, "John Otto: Trials and Trails," accompanies two other books he's penned on the monument and Grand Junction.

Interviewed for a story by the Sentinel's Al Look decades later, Chester said of Otto: "In all the time I trailed with John on trips in the rimrocks over the sides of Grand Mesa, I never saw him get angry at man or beast, never heard him utter an oath. He was tireless and a pleasing conversationalist, even if somewhat on the unusual side. He was educated to become a minister, but the old love of the wilds forbid it."

The men exchanged letters for years after leaving the Grand Valley — Otto affectionately referred to Chester as "Whooperino" in one of them — and they visited each other in San Jose, Calif., in 1950, when Otto was 79.

Mike Wiggins doesn't plan to return to live on the Front Range, where he grew up, anytime soon, and the monument is one reason why.

Letter from John Otto to former Daily Sentinel reporter Whipple Chester.
■ *Photo by Christopher Tomlinson*

Whipple Chester, left, and John Otto in 1950 visited in San Jose, Calif. Otto died two years later.
■ *Photo provided by Alan Kania*

Daily Sentinel journalists for the last 100 years have followed in Whipple Chester's footsteps, covering news events at Colorado National Monument. This photo by Jill Kaplan, published on Page One, April 7, 1982, shows National Park Service employees gathered to search for a missing hiker. ■ *Photo provided by The Daily Sentinel Collection/Museum of Western Colorado*

Homesteaders and John Otto

By Eileen O'Toole

There were things 28-year-old Agnes Honecker wanted in life: to be able to vote, to abolish liquor, to live a good, Catholic life, and to find a husband who believed the same.

Not having found those in Indiana working at a box factory, she set out West, arriving in Grand Junction on July 5, 1909, joining extended family already there.

One uncle, Joe Kiefer, was a good friend of John Otto, and the two of them took Honecker and her cousins hiking and camping on Grand Mesa and in Otto's park.

The park had no name yet, but Otto was busy building trails in preparation. The first time Honecker and her cousins climbed in the park they were hauled up by ropes. A few months later Otto had finished the trail. This time an unknown photographer captured their adventures in camp, on Liberty Cap and in Monument Canyon.

By this second trip, Honecker already had homesteaded 120 acres on the Redlands directly below the rock Otto called Jefferson Monument that now overlooks Tiara Rado Golf Course. She originally wanted the rock itself and the cliffs, canyons and benches surrounding it. Otto would have none of that — that was inside his park — so she settled for the land bordering it below.

After borrowing $25 from her dad and trading a building lot she owned in Indiana for her brother's labor to build her cabin, Honecker settled in to raise poultry, selling eggs and chicken to neighboring residents, including Otto.

Honecker sold her homestead in 1913 when she married Irish immigrant Joe deBlaquiere, who had 10 acres in Loma and worked as a clerk at the Mack railway station. Honecker in the end found what she wanted in life: Colorado women could vote, she never smashed a saloon but remained a teetotaler, and she married a man who generally agreed with her.

Eileen O'Toole is an artist, Redlands historian and a third-generation Redlands resident whose Grandmother Agnes (Honecker) deBlaquiere homesteaded there in 1909.

Fall foliage and monument ledges are reflected in this irrigated pasture off Broadway in the Redlands. The monument is surrounded by farms, ranches and houses — neighbors who value the stunning backdrop. ■ *Photo by Christopher Tomlinson*

Redlands pioneer Agnes Honecker wrote on the back of this picture: "Mr. and Mrs. Dittlinger, me, Mrs. Irving Miller, Bernard Hughes, John Otto, Edith Bath, Lena Bath, Uncle Joe (Kiefer) (in front of mule), Jim McConnell. One week's camping trip on the John Otto trail." ■ *Photo by unidentified photographer, 1909*

New Deal at Work

By Eric Sandstrom

The young men of the Civilian Conservation Corps worked in Colorado National Monument for years during the Great Depression, performing backbreaking labor with dynamite, sledgehammers and gigantic drills to clear the way for Rim Rock Drive.

These were the road builders, Americans of the Great Depression, who made the monument accessible to hundreds of thousands of visitors annually.

The CCC was one of the New Deal programs, along with the Works Project Administration (WPA) and Public Works Administration (PWA), which President Franklin D. Roosevelt established to revive the nation's economy while developing the country's roads, buildings, dams, canals and fire towers for national, state and metropolitan parks.

Roosevelt's plan called for men 18 to 25 years of age to enroll in these programs if they were destitute and willing to work hard for $30 a month.

The 22.5-mile Rim Rock Drive — and several sandstone buildings still in use — was built almost entirely by these young men whose

During the nine years that the Civilian Conservation Corps was active, more than 4,000 camps were established in all 48 states and four territories. ■ *Photo provided by National Park Service*

Civilian Conservation Corps license plate. ■ *Photo by Christopher Tomlinson*

A National Park Service Historic Rock Wall Crew repairs a retaining wall on Rim Rock Drive that was built in the 1930s. ■ *Photo by Christopher Tomlinson*

picks, shovels and sheer muscle power remain an inspiration to today's construction experts.

Leroy Lewis' parents were dirt-poor ranchers during the Depression, so he enrolled in the CCC at the age of 22 to become the breadwinner for his Grand Junction family. He remembered the Half Tunnel Tragedy in December of 1933. Nine of his co-workers were killed when a sandstone overhang sheared off. The accident buried most of them under tons of rock and sent others over the canyon lip and into the void. "For some of them, it was their first day of work," Lewis said.

From every monthly paycheck of $30, CCC workers were obligated to send $25 back to their families. FDR created the program to give the ailing economy a boost and to restore Americans' confidence in themselves and their country. From all accounts, it proved a remarkable success during its nine years of operation.

When the Japanese bombed Pearl Harbor in 1941, many of the 3 million CCC workers matriculated into the armed services.

Eric Sandstrom teaches at Mesa State College in Grand Junction and works summers as an interpretive park ranger at Colorado National Monument.

Crews in the 1930 blasted three tunnels for Rim Rock Drive — two on the west side and one on the east. ■*Photo provided by National Park Service*

Young men in the Depression-era federal work programs lived in man camps for six months to two years. ■*Photo provided by National Park Service*

Detonator used by construction crews during the building of Rim Rock Drive. ■*Photo by Christopher Tomlinson*

■ Photo provided by National Park Service

The following is from an oral history by Clint "Doc" Shoffner of Fort Collins, who joined the Civilian Conservation Corps in 1934 at 18 years old.

Shoffner went on to become a veterinarian. "It was a good experience," he said of his character-building time in the CCC. "I made use of it. I really did. It helped me when I got out into practice because it did teach me how to get along with people."

"When I was at the monument, I was a muleskinner. Building the road, it was done mostly by hand. At the time that I first got there I was using a 16-pound sledgehammer, breaking up rocks, and if you couldn't break them with a sledge, why then they called and blew 'em up with dynamite. Then you could move 'em. They got these little mine cars and would set the rails up where they were — cutting out a hill, for instance. They would set the rails up there and move up

the mine car. Then, with the mule I would hook onto that car and haul it down and dump it to get rid of the fill. Then I would pull the car back and the boys would fill it up again. As long as I used the mule I wouldn't even have to use a pick and shovel. It was great, except the mule was a mule that nobody could control, and they had had three or four guys trying to work with him. Finally, one morning the foreman lined us all up and said, "Does anybody here come from a ranch?" And, of course, you never volunteer anything. I said nothing. But the foreman and, incidentally, he was Irish, his name was Breen. He had such a brogue you could hardly understand him sometimes. But he looked down the line and said, "Shoffner, didn't you work on a ranch?" and I said, "yes." And he said, "Come here." I stepped out and he said, "Go get the mule." So the mule and I had to get acquainted. He was ornery as the dickens. He would kick you at the drop of a hat."

Wooden stairs gave road builders access to the top of the pile to start removing rock and debris on this stretch of Rim Rock Drive before the tunnel on the east approach. This particular road-cut wasn't completed until after the Korean War, sometime in the mid-1950s. Shortly thereafter the Serpents Trail was abandoned. ■ *Photo provided by National Park Service*

That same area in 2011 showed scant evidence of the massive amount of human effort that went into clearing the road. ■ *Photo by Christopher Tomlinson*

A Bay City Model No. 25 shovel alleviated some of the backbreaking work of monument road-building. Founded as Bay City Dredge Works in Bay City, Mich., in 1913, the company became Bay City Shovels in 1919. The line was discontinued in 1969. ■ *Photo provided by National Park Service*

Star of the Show

By Melinda Mawdsley

Even if people haven't experienced Colorado National Monument in person, they may have spotted its distinctive sandstone architecture in glossy advertisements or movie scenes.

Lana Turrou, a Grand Junction volunteer with Colorado's Office of Film, Television and Media, for more than 20 years has worked as a liaison, connecting advertisers and Hollywood to Mesa County locations, including the monument.

Rim Rock Drive, with its "S" curves and tunnels, is an appealing backdrop for some of the world's top car manufacturers, such as Audi, Chevrolet and Toyota.

But there is another reason commercial crews select the monument, and it has nothing to do with the rugged backdrop.

"They love afternoon, fluffy clouds, and we have an abundance of those," Turrou said.

Although car manufacturers most often have featured the monument, vehicles aren't the only products promoted.

In 1984 Kellogg filmed a commercial promoting its Start cereal, starring an elite British runner, 1984 Olympian Steve Cram, running along the monument's ridges before sitting down to his cereal breakfast.

The commercial aired exclusively in Europe.

Movies that have been filmed in the monument include the 1950 Western "Devil's Doorway" with Robert Taylor, the 1985 Kevin Costner film "American Flyers" and 2008's "The Lucky Ones" with Rachel McAdams and Tim Robbins.

Melinda Mawdsley is a features reporter for The Daily Sentinel and introduced her Midwestern farm family to Colorado National Monument, leaving them shocked that freestanding red-rock formations and canyons weren't just make-believe.

The 1950 Western "Devil's Doorway" sets up a classic range war between sheep and cattle ranchers, but with a twist for its time. Leading man Robert Taylor plays Lance Poole, an Indian with a Medal of Honor from the Battle of Gettysburg who just wants to raise cattle peacefully on his tribal lands. White sheep ranchers, however, want his fertile range for themselves. ■ *Photo provided by National Park Service*

In "American Flyers," Kevin Costner stars as sports physician Marcus Sommers, who convinces his unstable brother, David, to train with him for a bicycle race across the Rocky Mountains. The 1985 movie introduced many people to the strategy and athletic exertion of road bicycle racing.

■ Frank Dean photo provided by National Park Service

■ Photo by Christopher Tomlinson

Two brave (foolhardy?) adventurers stand on the precipice of Cold Shivers Point overlooking Columbus Canyon. Though there are various claims as to who named the overlook, there is no disputing why it was so named. Peering over the edge on perfectly stable, level ground can unleash a primal and sweat-inducing response to retreat before the bottom falls out.

Thanks

By Laurena Mayne Davis, editor

The creation of Colorado National Monument took 1.7 billion years of colliding land masses, chafing sands and abrasive, sediment-studded water.

The making of this book was no such monumental undertaking, but it did require the hard work, creative talents and generosity of dozens of people. Many of their bylines and photo credits appear on these pages. Others worked behind the scenes.

Monument Superintendent Joan Anzelmo and Michelle Wheatley, chief of interpretation and visitor services, made available hundreds of photos, documents and archaeological items in the monument's archives for our research. Because of that, readers of this book are able to see a Native American willow basket and the handwritten letters of monument booster John Otto. Though the credits state only "National Park Service," all of those items and photos are from the monument's archives.

Alan Kania's decades of research on Otto is without equal. He generously agreed to vet this book's historical content.

Museum of Western Colorado archivist and librarian Michael Menard helped pore over photos and clip files in the museum's Daily Sentinel collection.

Daily Sentinel Publisher Jay Seaton provided the impetus, budget and ongoing support from cover to cover, not to mention a well-developed appreciation for a compelling photo or turn of phrase.

Graphics Editor Robert García applied the same level of artistry to the design of this book that he has used to improve the aesthetics of Sentinel pages for 27 years.

This is, largely, a book of photos, and it would be less without the best from which to choose. All our staff photographers and many of our friends in the community provided their most spectacular images. Sentinel Chief Photographer Christopher Tomlinson, in particular, has made a personal study of photographing the monument. His body of work provides the storyboard for this book.

Dan Bennett, who works at the Sentinel in preproduction, improved

Although there are no permanent bodies of water in the monument, snowmelt runoff can pool temporarily, as with this small pond in No Thoroughfare Canyon. ■ *Photo by Ann Driggers*

historical images, scanning and sharpening them for best reproduction.

Copy Editor Dave Haynes proofread copy discerningly, and contributed his characteristic pithy and perfect headlines.

The talented journalists who wrote for this book did so while simultaneously producing the largest daily newspaper and the most popular news website in western Colorado. Guest writers were as giving of their time.

This book hopes to honor a community that strives to both engage and preserve the natural world.

May that endure at least another 1.7 billion years.

Epilogue

By Joan Anzelmo, Colorado National Monument superintendent

In the age of John Muir, some 1,000 miles from Yosemite Valley, a kindred spirit and fervent conservationist, John Otto, was dedicating himself to protecting and promoting the land that today we know as Colorado National Monument. Otto built the first trails into this rugged landscape to reach the glorious red rock canyons. He dreamed of building a road high above the majestic cliffs where once only birds could fly.

Otto was advocating for national park protection of this stunning Colorado canyon country on the heels of the very first national parks being established by Congress in the late 1800s and early 1900s.

In today's daunting world, national parks have even broader meaning and value to society. National parks unite us as a country and gather us together around the globe. They tell our story as a people: the glory and the shame, the triumphs and the tragedies. They celebrate America's incomparable landscapes. They provide places for sublime peace and contemplation and places for adventurous exploration. Their reservoirs of scientific knowledge and discoveries are helping cure diseases, solve crimes and are recording the beginnings of the Earth to the present day changes in our planet.

■ Photo by Gretel Daugherty

It is no wonder that Wallace Stegner said: "National parks are the best idea we ever had. Absolutely American, absolutely democratic, they reflect us at our best rather than our worst."

We need them now more than ever.

A masonry crew uses a Bobcat for retaining-wall repair. Mason Charlie Runde helps guide a stone into place along the west end of Rim Rock Drive. ■ *Photo by Christopher Tomlinson*

Crews in the 1960s line a tunnel with gunite — dry cement mixed with water that is blasted by pneumatic pressure from a gun, hence the term "gun"-ite. ■ *Photo provided by National Park Service*

The three Rim Rock Drive tunnels are 182, 236 and 530 feet in length. ■ *Photo provided by National Park Service*

Paving Rim Rock Drive in the early 1950s greatly increased motorist accessibility to the monument.
■ *Photo provided by National Park Service*

Colorado National Monument is roughly 10 miles long, varying from three miles to six miles in width.
■ *Photo provided by National Park Service*

Monument tunnel repair in 1977. ■ *Photo provided by Daily Sentinel Collection/Museum of Western Colorado*

Motor vehicle headlights and taillights trail neon streaks in this 30-second time exposure photograph taken with film on Rim Rock Drive. The dots are bicycle headlights. ▪ *Photo by Dean Humphrey*

An Aug. 8, 1968, record rainstorm washed out three sections of Rim Rock Drive, including this section between the two tunnels on the west end. The 2.01 inches of rain overpowered a culvert, leaving the deluge to funnel right down the uppermost tunnel. ■ *Photo provided by National Park Service*

Restoration to the west end of Rim Rock Drive, shown here in 2011, was accomplished with 130,000 cubic yards of fill at a repair cost of $475,000, and that's in 1969 dollars. ■ *Photo by Christopher Tomlinson*

Classic Rock: Best of the Stones
By Rachel Sauer

History in hyper-speed is an opera, a bombastic diorama of crashing continents, mountains heaving and valleys buckling. It's howling winds that erase vertical miles and rushing water that carves with a circuitous, relentless precision. It's life that lives and dies and lies down in stone.

Slowed to real time, history is only evident in hindsight, a billion or more years written in the layers and fissures and undulations of Colorado National Monument. In this place, eons are painted with a geological palette.

What now are flat-bottomed redrock canyons have several times been sawtooth mountain ranges, been buried beneath an inland sea and been scoured by drifting sand dunes, said geologist Bill Hood. They are evidence of change as an inexorable constant.

"The black stuff at the bottom of the canyons is 1.7 billion years old, a third of the age of Earth," Hood said. "It formed when Colorado and adjacent areas south moved north and collided with ancestral North America at the Colorado/Wyoming state line. It created a mountain range like the Himalayas."

That was followed by millions of years of erosion, exposing the metamorphic and igneous hearts of the shrinking, flattening mountains. Then the sea invaded, depositing layers of sediment, and eons later retreated.

South America collided with North America, creating the ancestral Rocky Mountains and Uncompahgre Plateau.

And always, the erosion and upheaval continued. Each layer of color exposed in the monument's cliffs today tells the story of millions of years. The red rocks at the base of the cliffs record a time when this area was close to the equator. The wide band of rusty Wingate sandstone that makes up the widest swath

Opposite – Colorado National Monument is part of the immense Colorado Plateau, red rock terrain that spans the Four Corners region of the Southwest – Colorado, Utah, Arizona and New Mexico. The Colorado Plateau has the greatest concentration of national parks and monuments in the United States, including Grand Canyon, Arches and Mesa Verde national parks, and Colorado, Dinosaur and Natural Bridges national monuments.
■ *Photo by Christopher Tomlinson*

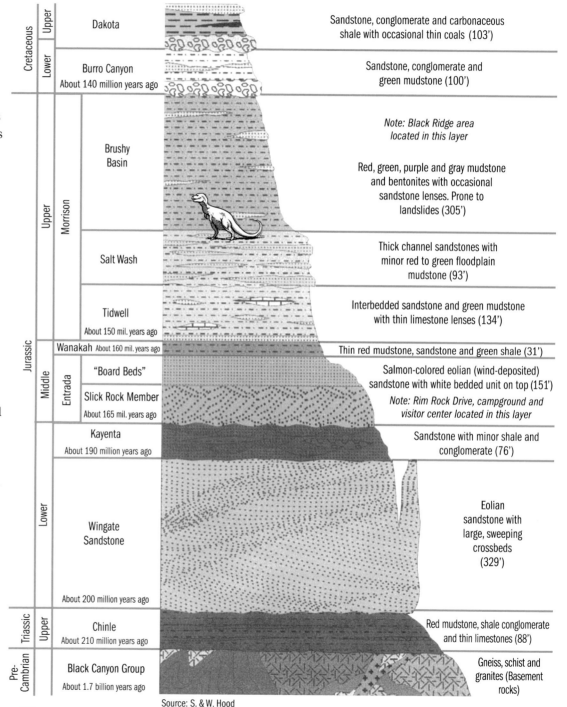

Cretaceous	Upper	Dakota	Sandstone, conglomerate and carbonaceous shale with occasional thin coals (103')
	Lower	Burro Canyon — About 140 million years ago	Sandstone, conglomerate and green mudstone (100')
Jurassic	Upper — Morrison	Brushy Basin	Note: Black Ridge area located in this layer — Red, green, purple and gray mudstone and bentonites with occasional sandstone lenses. Prone to landslides (305')
		Salt Wash	Thick channel sandstones with minor red to green floodplain mudstone (93')
		Tidwell — About 150 mil. years ago	Interbedded sandstone and green mudstone with thin limestone lenses (134')
		Wanakah About 160 mil. years ago	Thin red mudstone, sandstone and green shale (31')
	Middle — Entrada	"Board Beds"	Salmon-colored eolian (wind-deposited) sandstone with white bedded unit on top (151')
		Slick Rock Member — About 165 mil. years ago	Note: Rim Rock Drive, campground and visitor center located in this layer
	Lower	Kayenta — About 190 million years ago	Sandstone with minor shale and conglomerate (76')
		Wingate Sandstone — About 200 million years ago	Eolian sandstone with large, sweeping crossbeds (329')
Triassic	Upper	Chinle — About 210 million years ago	Red mudstone, shale conglomerate and thin limestones (88')
Pre-Cambrian		Black Canyon Group — About 1.7 billion years ago	Gneiss, schist and granites (Basement rocks)

Source: S. & W. Hood

of cliff face represents North America's northward journey. That's topped by the Kayenta Formation and, on top of that, Entrada sandstone that's evidence of sand blowing in from dunes around a shallow sea in present-day Utah.

As Earth's plates pushed and buckled the land and the wind sculpted it, water carved it. The Colorado River took away six inches of sediment every 1,000 years, Hood said, and continues to do so. Smaller creeks did their work, too, carving alleys of canyons.

The change continues now, an ongoing push and pull that will be evident in 10 million years. But today in the monument, hardy young plants grow in 200-million-year-old soil, evidence that through the slow change, life endures.

Rachel Sauer, a Daily Sentinel reporter and amateur paleontologist, wouldn't mind a fossilized future alongside the Grand Valley's dinosaurs.

Potholes are natural bowls in sandstone that collect rainwater and windblown sediment. Even small potholes contain important ecosystems. They harbor organisms that are able to survive long periods of dehydration, and also serve as a breeding ground for many high-desert amphibians and insects. ■ *Photo by Christopher Tomlinson*

Colorado National Monument is 32 square miles of canyon and plateau country, situated on the edge of the Uncompahgre Uplift. At its highest point, the monument soars more than 2,000 feet above the valley floor. The top of Independence Monument is 5,739 feet in elevation. ■ *Photo by Christopher Tomlinson*

The Making of a Monolith ■ *Graphic by Robert García*

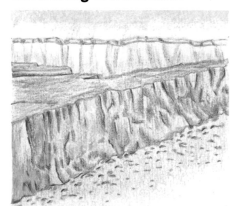

At one time, Independence Monument was part of an expansive wall between Wedding and Monument canyons.

The power of weathering and erosion gradually expanded these canyons, and the dividing wall became thinner and began to break down.

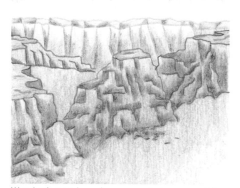

Weathering and erosion proceeded more rapidly in places where rock was most vulnerable — along its natural fractures. Eventually the wall was breached and parts of it collapsed.

Today, a remnant of the once solid rock wall survives as Independence Monument, a free-standing monolith. It too, will eventually succumb to the ravages of time and weather.

Daily Sentinel Graphics Editor Robert García can trace his family's roots in Colorado to the 1850s. He has lived in various areas of the state, and the monument is one reason why he has remained here since 1984.

Ancient Life
By Dennis Webb

When retired paleontologist George Callison looks at Colorado National Monument and its surrounding environs, he imagines a lush, stream-filled landscape teeming with life.

Callison's mind conjures Jurassic times, when now-extinct animals such as dinosaurs and flying reptiles mingled with many others that survive today, from lizards to mammals to turtles and crocodiles.

"It was a pretty exciting time and a lot of us are sorry that we can't go back and see it," Callison said.

What paleontologists can't see in person, they've been able to reconstruct from major fossil discoveries in nearby areas such as Fruita, Rabbit Valley and Dry Mesa near Delta. Colorado National Monument has been slower to yield its paleontological secrets, but that's starting to change.

In 2005, a monument visitor found what appear to be the tracks of multiple turtles some 150 million years old. They're only the second set of turtle tracks to be found in the Jurassic-Period Morrison Formation in North America.

The Jurassic Period is called the "Age of Reptiles" for their proliferation in an increasingly warm and humid climate. On rainy and foggy days in Colorado National Monument, it's easy, still, to imagine their reign there. ■ *Photo by Christopher Tomlinson*

In September 2010, John Foster, paleontologist with the Dinosaur Journey Museum in Fruita, stumbled across fossilized lizard tracks while at the monument to remove the turtle tracks after the slab containing them broke off a cliff. The lizard tracks are the first ever found in the Morrison Formation.

Earlier that same month, a monument employee found a three-toed dinosaur track.

"There's no question there's a lot more tracks up there," said Foster. "It's all a matter of getting up there and looking for them and putting in enough time to find the rare ones."

One unusual find involved footprints left by a large sauropod. It had stepped several feet into mud, making postholes that filled with sand. That sand hardened and was preserved in the form of pillars when the mud eroded away, leaving not just footprints but lower-leg castings.

Foster said another notable discovery was a Jurassic lungfish tooth, found in 2004.

The monument's protective status and relative inaccessibility have limited fossil finds, but also made it harder for people to make off with fossils, Foster said.

Callison said lower locales surrounding the monument have been more dissected by erosion that exposed large amounts of fossils to paleontologists. The geological uplifting of the monument helped lead to that erosion.

"So in an indirect way the monument has made all these peripheral discoveries possible," Callison said.

Dennis Webb is a Daily Sentinel reporter who moved to Colorado 22 years ago for the mountains, only to fall equally in love with its canyon country.

This three-toed dinosaur fossilized track measures some 10 inches long and was found by a Colorado National Monument employee. It's yet unknown if the track was made by a plant- or meat-eating dinosaur.
■ *Photo by Christopher Tomlinson*

John Foster, paleontologist for Dinosaur Journey Museum in Fruita, discovered tiny fossilized lizard tracks on the monument. ■ *Photo by Dean Humphrey*

The Bone Hunter

By Laurena Mayne Davis

Monday through Friday, Al Look was the suit-and-tie advertising manager for The Daily Sentinel during much of the 20th century.

Weekends, however, he laced up hiking boots and traipsed western Colorado backcountry as amateur archaeologist, anthropologist, geologist and paleontologist.

He also published, with folksy flair, several books about his wide-ranging interests — everything from the Hopi snake dance to uranium to dinosaurs.

Two archaeological sites are named for him, as is the *Sparactolambda looki*, a tusked, piglike animal whose fossilized skull Look and his son, Al Jr., discovered in 1937.

"Bone hunters never know what fossil their pick will unearth next, to take its place in the orderly scheme of once living things," Look wrote in his 1951 book "In My Back Yard." "To open a grave 60 million years old and be the first human being in all eternity to look at a brand new and unsuspected species of animal life is a thrill difficult to describe. Fossils are the historical documents from which the unwritten story of life is read."

Laurena Mayne Davis, managing editor for The Daily Sentinel, bonded with the monument during a 22.6-mile Rim Rock Run replete with snow, rain, spontaneous waterfalls and the elevating scent of wet pinyon pines.

Opposite —
Snow traces the filigreed branches of a downed tree on a canyon rim on the west end of Colorado National Monument. ■ *Photo by Christopher Tomlinson*

Al Look made exploration of the natural world in his backyard his passionate avocation. ■ *Photo provided by Museum of Western Colorado*

Overleaf — Seen from Monument Canyon View, to the right of Independence Monument is The Island, in the back, and the crown of Kissing Couple, in front. ■ *Photo by Christopher Tomlinson*

39

Desert in Bloom

By Tess Furey

Look beyond the obvious and you'll find a fascinating cast of floral characters on Colorado National Monument, from native grasses, shrubs, desert succulents and wildflowers to lush hanging gardens and old-growth trees.

Be amazed at the pinyon-juniper woodlands, which dominate the monument.

Some of the junipers are Methuselahs. Using tree-ring dating, Deborah Kennard, assistant professor of environmental science at Mesa State College, has found junipers that have been on this planet nearly 1,000 years. Junipers with the most twisted and misshapen trunks are likely very old. They employ a technique — shifting all water, nutrients and sap to one side of the tree, causing the other side to wither — in order to survive.

Pinyons have infrequent seed harvests because of the cold winters and arid summers. When they do produce a bumper crop, pinyon jays and squirrels have a feast.

In spring and summer prickly pears put on a colorful show with large, waxy, yellow, crimson-bronze, pink and violet flowers. They are an important food source and burrowing spot for scrambling rodents.

Feast your eyes on the wildflowers. Seeps, springs and waterfalls support micro-climates, and cliffs give protection and warmth for sub-tropical growth, such as the orchids, horsetails and ferns. Pretty and prolific varieties are a kaleidoscope of the trumpet-shaped penstemon, buckwheat and crypantha.

Flowers in the mustard family and sunflowers bloom from summer to fall, said Kennard. Along Rim Rock Drive,

Desert four o'clock

Pinyon and juniper cover 75 percent of the mesa tops in Colorado National Monument. Junipers, such as this one, produce a cone that looks like a blue, wax-covered berry. These cones are poisonous to most animals but a rich food source to others. ■ *Photo by Christopher Tomlinson*

This cross-section of a Utah juniper tree from Colorado National Monument has more than 950 rings, with one ring for each year of its life. It is one of the oldest trees studied in the park. ■ *Photo by Deborah Kennard*

Opposite —
Globe mallow
■ *Photos by
Christopher
Tomlinson*

evening primrose blooms on cooler evenings, pollinated by night-flying insects. Desert four o'clocks sport thick, waxy coverings to reduce water loss.

Admire the resiliency of cacti and succulents. Exposed to freezing winters, unlike their Southwestern compatriots, their will to live causes them to reduce the moisture in their tissues to the point they shrivel, thus surviving frigid temperatures without freezing. In spring, they are reborn.

Tread not on the off-trail soil crust. Formed over many years by moss, lichen, cyanobacteria algae and fungi, the crust hosts an environment where seeds can grow. A footprint can erase decades of growth. Non-native invasive species also threaten the monument. Although the environment is pristine by many standards, Eurasian cheatgrass is probably the biggest threat to natural flora, Kennard said.

Prickly pear cactus

And give a hand to the supporting cast, single-leaf ash, mountain mahogany, rabbitbrush, Mormon tea, yucca, serviceberry and sagebrush, which support the complete ecosystem.

In all, at least 418 species of vascular plants have been identified in the park, and biologists are bound to discover more.

Tess Furey, a newcomer mesmerized by the raw beauty of the American West, is an avid student of the landscape, lore and pioneer spirit.

Indian paintbrush

Paper flower

Desert pink

Sego lily

Sego lily

Milkvetch ■ *Photos by Christopher Tomlinson*

For a few months every spring the high desert's demure earthtone pallette is spattered with rainbow wildflowers. The more moisture, the more flowers, as was the case in 2010 when the desert's usual frugal flowering was replaced with fields abloom in petals of every hue.

Overleaf — The first light of morning shimmers on the red canyon walls of Colorado National Monument. ■ *Photo by Christopher Tomlinson*

"Claret Cups" ■
*Oil painting by
John Lintott*

All Creatures Great and Small

By Dave Buchanan

Visitors to Colorado National Monument aren't sheepish when it comes to mountain lions.

"The most inquiries we get is about predators," said Michelle Wheatley, chief of interpretation and visitor services for the monument. "So many people want to know about mountain lions."

Not just about, but also where they might see one of the elusive, tawny-coated beasts.

While sightings of mountain lions are rare, Wheatley said it's much easier for her to point visitors toward the other half of the relationship, the monument's plentiful, popular and visible desert bighorn sheep.

"In general, that's the most-popular animal," Wheatley said of the herd that was started in 1979. "People love to see sheep."

Some of the best places to view bighorn sheep are along the cliffs in Fruita Canyon and trails in Monument Canyon and near the base of Independence Monument.

Desert bighorn sheep, a subspecies of bighorn sheep, are particularly adapted to an arid environment. They have longer legs, smaller bodies, a lighter coat and the ability to go without water for days or even weeks. Once on the brink of extinction, a small herd was reintroduced to Colorado National Monument in 1979. Today there are more than 230 sheep in the Black Ridge Herd. At any given time there are some 40-plus desert bighorn in the monument. ■ *Photos by Richard Janson*

But charismatic megafauna are only part of the monument's wildlife story.

"There are a few unique species in the monument people should watch for," said Dusty Perkins, program manager for the Northern Colorado Plateau Network, which monitors ecosystems in 16 national parks in four states. "For instance, one of the only spots on the Colorado Plateau to see the red-spotted toad is in the monument."

Budding herpetologists also focus on the neon-bright collared lizard, with its daffodil-yellow head and lime-green body. But focus fast, because this foot-long carnivorous reptile can run on its hind legs up to 15 miles per hour.

The monument's variety of ecosystems, from the desert grasslands around the base to the pinyon-juniper woodlands at the top, along with a few pockets of willows and cottonwood trees, attracts a diverse population of birds and birders.

Perkins said birds, in addition to their immense public appeal, are vital indicators of ecosystem health.

A couple of species, including mourning dove, show some early signs of decline. Several other species are showing consistent annual increases: black phoebe, black-throated sparrow and dusky flycatcher, all of which might be seen in the monument.

Daily Sentinel outdoors writer Dave Buchanan first visited Colorado National Monument when it was 45 years old. Both have aged quite gracefully since, thank you very much.

The midget-faded rattlesnake, a subspecies of the Western rattlesnake, is the only venomous snake found in the monument. They are non-aggressive and will avoid human contact. ■ *Photo by Christopher Tomlinson*

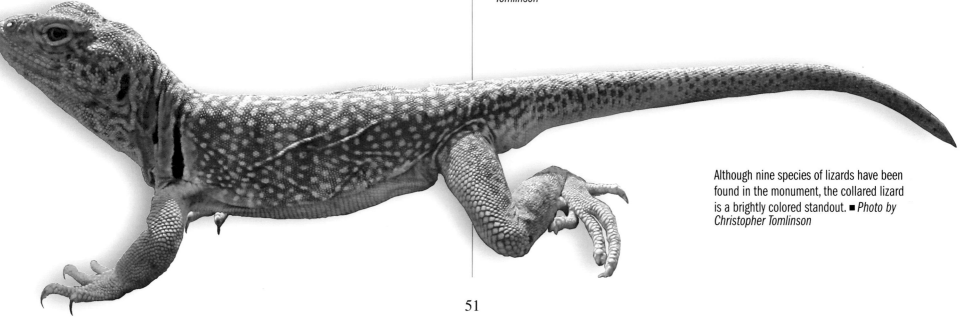

Although nine species of lizards have been found in the monument, the collared lizard is a brightly colored standout. ■ *Photo by Christopher Tomlinson*

A young giant desert hairy scorpion, less than half an inch long, warms itself in the desert sun. It could grow to six inches in adulthood. ■ *Photo by Christopher Tomlinson*

Opposite — A black-chinned hummingbird eyes a distant intruder (with a long-range lens) from her nest in a pinyon pine near Highland View. Black-chinned hummingbirds are migratory, returning in April to range in open pinyon-juniper woodland, riparian and even suburban areas. By the first of May, males build soft, spongy cups from the plant down of thistle, cattails and milkweed and wrap the nests securely in spider webs. Minute nests often are only three to six feet off the ground, on tree branches, sagebrush and even tall weeds. ■ *Photo by Christopher Tomlinson*

Tiny tracks reveal the snowy passage of a small rodent near Otto's Trail. ■ *Photo by Christopher Tomlinson*

This male collared lizard bore his burden for science — and it looked a lot like a fanny pack. Bulky radio transmitters were state of the art in 1989 when they were used to track the activities of 12 lizards in the monument. Researchers from the University of Windsor in Canada over the course of a summer studied the movements of not only collared, but side-blotched, fence, sagebrush and tree lizards. Radio signals were received with antennae that looked similar to television "rabbit ears" and recorded on a radio tracking device the size of a toaster, which was strapped to the chest of a researcher in the field. That same summer, various scientists studied plant life, insects and arthropods, bats, a nesting pair of peregrine falcons and air quality. Daily Sentinel photographer Christopher Tomlinson was there on that brisk late-spring day to photograph the lizard-trackers at work. ■ *Photo by Christopher Tomlinson*

A common raven fends off a marauding golden eagle over Red Canyon. Seen throughout the monument, common ravens are members of the crow family. They have a wide range of vocalizations, including the ability to mimic. They mate for life and defend their territory together. ■ *Photo by Christopher Tomlinson*

A Rare Find

By Emily Anderson

It was discovered in Colorado over a hundred years ago and has been spotted flitting all over western North America. But there was no mention of *Lithariapteryx abroniaeella* again in Colorado until a study in Colorado National Monument.

That may be because no one was looking for the tiny, silver-scaled moth with orange markings, according to Paul Opler. Or maybe they didn't see it; the moth has a wingspan of 1 centimeter.

Opler, a Loveland entomologist and Colorado State University professor, brought the micromoth back into notoriety in the state while he presided over a 10-year study of moths and butterflies in the monument. He found a plant near the visitor center filled with *Lithariapteryx abroniaeella* caterpillars and raised the moths to maturity on the Front Range.

Opler observed that the *Lithariapteryx abroniaeella* fly in the daytime and live in purple-flowered plants, and that their orange-and-black markings resemble the eyes of a small jumping spider. Opler and University of California-Berkeley professor Jerry Powell detailed its characteristics in the book "Moths of Western North America."

Opler said there are "at least seven or eight" moth species found only in the monument or found in just one or two other places in the world.

Emily Anderson, a reporter for The Daily Sentinel, has hiked every trail in Colorado National Monument since moving to the Grand Valley from Iowa in 2006. Despite her mother's fears, she has never fallen off the monument.

LITHARIAPTERYX ABRONIAEELLA

Opposite — Morning fog blankets the northwest side of the monument. ■ *Photo by Dean Humphrey*

■ *Pen and ink watercolor by Suzie Garner*

Where the Buffalo Roamed
By Tammy Gemaehlich

Bison — an iconic symbol of the Old West — once roamed the canyons of Colorado National Monument, menacing hikers and neighbors, and scaring off native wildlife.

John Otto introduced bison to the park in 1926 as a tourist attraction. Otto's P.T. Barnum approach to park promotions was well-meaning, but over time the multiplying herd took its toll.

Roaming primarily in Wedding, Ute and Red canyons, the buffalo trampled grasses they didn't consume, causing extreme erosion. They overran desert bighorn sheep habitat, stripped vegetative cover and invaded watering holes.

In February 1983, then-Monument Superintendent Dennis Huffman declared in a Daily Sentinel story that the range wasn't capable of supporting the buffalo herd, then numbering around 37. A Soil Conservation Service study indicated the range on the monument was under severe stress because of the buffalo.

"The crux of the matter is that the range is seriously being deteriorated," Huffman said. "The only thing besides feeding them like in a zoo is to get rid of them."

The monument thinned its buffalo herd over six months, leaving about 10 in the park. The remaining buffalo were quarantined in Olathe to determine if they were infected with brucellosis, a bacterial infection.

Found to be healthy, some of the animals were given to the Southern Utes. The rest were transported to Badlands National Park in South Dakota, joining a herd of about 400 already there in a more natural environment for buffalo.

Tammy Gemaehlich, an avid mountain biker and hiker, has been with The Daily Sentinel for 19 years and received a marriage proposal from her future husband while hiking the monument's Liberty Cap Trail.

John Otto treated the buffalo he transplanted into the monument as pets. Here he approaches a favorite bull. ∎ *Photo provided by National Park Service*

Opposite — The last of the monument's buffalo were herded up and removed from the park in 1983 and 1984. ∎ *Photo provided by Daily Sentinel Collection/ Museum of Western Colorado*

Overleaf — Homes, farms and businesses skirt the monument on three sides, making it not only a national treasure of public land for tourists, but an extended backyard for many Grand Valley residents. ∎ *Photo by Christopher Tomlinson*

Monument Within a Monument

By Dave Haynes

Take a good, long look at Independence Monument.

Now close your eyes for a moment. Open them and take another look, and you will not notice that the monument has changed. It has.

In the blink of a human eye, a grain or two of sand, or a handful of them, have fallen from their high perch. By the time you finish reading this sentence, another grain, or a handful, will have given in to gravity's pull and joined the dunes at the base of the spire.

This monument within a monument is disappearing before your eyes.

Wind and water are the rivals of this rock and all those like it. The monolith that now towers over Monument Canyon will endure nature's onslaught for a few hundred thousand more years, then wither to a stump, then a nub, then a dune.

The most-recognizable icon of Colorado National Monument is doomed, in a fittingly ironic twist, by the same elements that created it.

The thick, compressed sand deposits from which Independence Monument was carved accumulated over eons across what is now the Colorado Plateau.

Wind pushed uncountable billions of tons of sand across an arid landscape, creating giant dunes.

These sediments had leveled and compressed into a large wall of Wingate sandstone that separated Monument and Wedding canyons.

Visitors at Independence Monument View keep tabs on climbers making their way up Independence Monument on the Fourth of July.
■ *Photo by Christopher Tomlinson*

Opposite — Independence Monument bisects the morning sun in Wedding Canyon.
■ *Photo by Christopher Tomlinson*

An aerial view shows Rim Rock Drive to the left and Grand View Point pullout. ■ *Photo by Christopher Tomlinson*

A newer deposit of minerals — the Kayenta formation — overlay the less-dense Wingate rock. Here and there a rivulet of water formed a crease in the capstone, then a crack, then a fissure. The rock eroded, crumbled, split and fell. Water seeped into the cracks, froze and expanded, pushing on the rock and accelerating its demise.

Millions of years passed, and the irresistible forces of water and gravity cut through the Wingate like a blade through wood. Entire walls of sandstone eroded and collapsed, leaving here and there free-standing columns, like Independence, whose only allies against the destructive will of nature were their hard Kayenta caps.

These durable quartz slabs of capstone are merely postponing the inevitable. They can only protect their Wingate bases for so long. Time and the elements will wear them down and they will surrender — one grain of sand, or a handful, at a time.

Dave Haynes is a native and lifelong resident of western Colorado whose love of wide-open spaces drives him to explore every nook of the great Southwest, usually in the company of an adventurous border collie/Aussie shepherd mix named Molly.

First to scale Independence Monument on the Fourth of July and plant Old Glory at the pinnacle was John Otto, in 1911, but others have taken up the cause. Now every Independence Day members of the Mesa County Technical Search and Rescue Team take up climbers for a small fee as a fundraiser for the volunteer organization. The flag flies one week, then climbers retrieve the flag and stow the flagpole under a rock ledge. ■ *Photos by Christopher Tomlinson*

On the Trail
By Bill Haggerty

Miles of trails traverse Colorado National Monument. Two trails, however, are well-known for plunging hikers into the heart of canyonland country or ascending them to a raven's-eye view of the scenery.

Winding through a spectacular canyon, Monument Canyon Trail leads to many of the major rock structures for which the monument is famous. The immense sandstone monoliths of Independence Monument, Kissing Couple and the Coke Ovens tower overhead.

Serpents Trail, on the other hand, twists up the spine of the monument to look down on the rest of the world. It is a remaining section of the larger Trail of the Serpent roadway, built in the early 1900s, and was used as the main road onto Glade Park and Pinyon Mesa until the east end of Rim Rock Drive opened. The trail is 1.75 miles one way with 16 switchbacks. It climbs steadily from east to west, from an elevation of 5,060 to 5,760 feet.

Views overlooking the Grand Valley from this trail are spectacular, but hikers should watch their step and their children at overlooks and steep dropoffs. Occasionally hikers will stumble across a coyote, bobcat or desert bighorn sheep track. Now and again they may even see one of those majestic bighorns.

On either trail, as the light changes throughout the day, hikers will be mesmerized, enchanted and enthralled by the trails of the monument.

Outdoor columnist Bill Haggerty has lived, hiked, skied, biked and played in Colorado all his life and lives at the base of Colorado National Monument, which is way better than living at the base of the Washington National Monument.

Opposite — Education Ranger Annie Runde leads a group of schoolchildren on a hike of Canyon Rim Trail below the visitor center. Just minutes away from the metropolitan Grand Valley, Colorado National Monument is a popular and accessible field trip and camping destination for local youth groups. ■ *Photo by Christopher Tomlinson*

Devils Kitchen Trail is a family-friendly hike of 1½ miles roundtrip. ■ *Photo by Christopher Tomlinson*

Devils Kitchen Trail leads to a rock "room" walled with sandstone sentinels. ■ *Photo by Christopher Tomlinson*

Canyon Rim Trail, near the visitor center, is a flat mile of breathtaking views of Wedding Canyon. Pipe Organ is centered in front. ■ *Photo by Christopher Tomlinson*

Colorado National Monument hiking trails are well-marked at trail heads with maps, levels of difficulty, lengths and other helpful information. Marked trails range from a quarter-mile to 8½ miles. The shortest is Window Rock and the longest is No Thoroughfare. ■ *Photo by Christopher Tomlinson*

Mark Sills playfully tosses his delighted daughter, Nerea Sills, on a family hike of Otto's Trail. ■ *Photo by Maria Sills*

Siblings Jack, Tom and Ellen Gummere share a hug while taking in the view, circa 1949. ■ *Photo by Ida Gummere*

This free climber in Devils Kitchen searches for hand holds and foot holds in small indents and ledges of the rock face. ■ *Photo by Christopher Tomlinson*

■ *Photo by Dean Humphrey*

Run to Glory
By Ann Driggers

He stands tall on a rocky perch at the mouth of Ute Canyon, a solitary desert bighorn peering down as I run below on rolling singletrack plowing through a sea of sagebrush. My steady pace falters as I gaze up in wonder. He's not as impressed with me as I with him and stares me down.

Under his watchful eye I continue along the canyon floor to its head where rocky switchbacks wind through precipitous rock walls and spit me out and onto the rim. Here I look back from whence I came, deep into the U-shaped canyon flanked with its sheer cliffs while a red-tailed hawk soars above me.

Ute Canyon is a favorite trail for running. Old Gordon's, Liberty Cap and Monument Canyon are as well. Sometimes I link a combination of trails and run for hours, pounding out the miles, reveling in both the beauty and the workout. But most times I run, I have no plan other than to immerse myself in the glory of the red rock cathedral that is my backyard.

I run game trails that vanish and reappear in the red earth, weaving between pinyon and juniper. I clamber up streambeds, over jumbled rock or sink in the wet sand, marveling at springs and clusters of lush vegetation in the desert.

I run with the ebb and flow of the seasons and its weather. The searing heat of summer is avoided with a pre-dawn start or late afternoon when north-facing walls cast cool shadows and fluffy afternoon clouds build into granite thunderheads. Rain drums down, pooling, swelling, overflowing until a flash flood roars out of gaping canyon mouths. I like to run after the rain, the smell of sage and damp earth rising, the water sinking through the sand, the canyon floor cleansed, rocks moved, trees snapped, my trail vanished.

As the heat abates, blazing cottonwoods fill the canyons with autumn color, a harvest moon slides behind the rim and the canyon walls echo with the howls of coyotes. In winter the red rock is glazed with ice and shimmers under a cloak of white. I still run, leaving my prints in the snow next to those of the coyotes, sheep and other wildlife.

Snows melt, the desert greens and flourishes with new life.

Rim Rock Run, started in 1993, was a 22.6-mile race along the length of Rim Rock Drive. In 2009 it was extended to a full marathon and renamed Rim Rock Marathon. It's a road race, but with the relative solitude, spectacular views and lung-bursting changes in elevation often associated with trail running. As one runner explained, "This is a race you run for the experience, not the personal record." ■ *Photo by Christopher Tomlinson*

Nesting quail and an abundance of dazzling wildflowers herald the arrival of spring. Joy in this place of exquisite natural beauty is renewed again. I run.

Ann Driggers, a weekend warrior outdoor adventurist, lives in the shadow of Colorado National Monument where she hikes, bikes, skis, climbs and, most often, runs to her heart's content.

71

Riding the Rim
By Allen Gemaehlich

Looking through a car windshield is not the only way to enjoy the views along Rim Rock Drive. Cyclists enjoy the physical challenge and the natural grandeur.

"What makes it so fun is it has beautiful scenery," said former professional cyclist Scott Mercier of Fruita. "You are earning the climbs, and the pavement is in great shape. You really get to go pretty high speeds and it's pretty safe. The climb is not so hard it's putting you out of business. The reward is you scream down. It's the way cycling is meant to be."

Cycling the monument became so popular it helped lure the first major pro cycling event to the United States in 1975.

■ *Photo by Christopher Tomlinson*

Celestial Seasonings herbal tea company of Boulder started the Red Zinger Bicycle Classic to promote its new tea. One of the stages included the "Tour of the Moon"

Riders in The Denver Post Ride the Rockies pause at Independence Monument View in 2010. Colorado's premier cycling event is a six- to seven-day ride, with differing routes every year, among some of the most striking scenery Colorado has to offer. ■ *Photo by Christopher Tomlinson*

The peloton attacks Rim Rock Drive in the 1986 Tour of the Moon. A stage of the Coors International Bicycle Classic, the Tour of the Moon was named for the otherworldly landscape of Colorado National Monument. ■ *Photo by Christopher Tomlinson*

Tour of the Moon riders snake their way up the east side of Colorado National Monument in 1986. Coors was the race's second sponsor. The first sponsor, Celestial Seasonings, started the race in 1975 and named it after its Red Zinger tea. The Red Zinger and Coors Classic stage races showcased world-class men and women's cycling throughout California, Colorado, Hawaii, Nevada and Wyoming. The race was considered the fourth-biggest race on the world cycling calendar. ■ *Photo by Christopher Tomlinson*

■ *Logo designed by Robert García*

over Rim Rock Drive. It was the first bicycle race to close a national park for the event. Coors Brewery took over the title sponsorship in 1980 and the race continued through 1988. It featured Tour de France winners Greg LeMond and Bernard Hinault.

The Tour of the Moon stage was featured in the 1985 Warner Brothers movie "American Flyers," starring Kevin Costner.

"Cycling at that point was a niche sport as it still is, but it was becoming more involved in America," Mercier said. "The Tour of the Moon was one of the big stages in American pro cycling."

The monument's canyonlands are a distinguishing draw for cyclists all over the world.

"It's so unique," Mercier said. "In Europe, you have the Alps. Sure, we have the Rockies, but they don't compare to the Alps. We've got beautiful mountains, but they have that in Europe. They don't have anything at all that compares to the high-desert, sandstone cliffs that you can ride your bike through."

It's not only races that have drawn cyclists to the monument.

"There's nothing more spectacular than an early-morning ride when it's almost dark when you start out and by the time you're two-thirds of the way up the sun is cresting up over the Mesa," Mercier said. "Your shadows are 100 feet long. It has all the elements of a classic ride and very little traffic to contend with."

Allen Gemaehlich enjoys going on biking adventures, whether it's the White Rim Trail through Canyonlands National Park or riding his mountain bike over Colorado National Monument.

Not every cycling event on Colorado National Monument is a race of world-class athletes. The Tour of the Valley is sponsored by Community Hospital in Grand Junction and includes a 100-mile route and options of shorter, family-friendly routes. ■ *Photo by Robert García*

The first leg of the 2010 Ride the Rockies 523-mile tour showcased Rim Rock Drive. ■ *Photo by Christopher Tomlinson*

What's in a Name?

By Eric Sandstrom

As the monument's first custodian, John Otto named many formations. It was almost as though these familiar rocky towers were his children in need of an identity. Needle's Eye, King Apple's Castle and Temple Rock were all his doing.

Monument Canyon's iconic 450-foot spire was christened Independence by Otto. He called a distinctive beehive-shaped formation Haystacks. It later was renamed Coke Ovens, possibly by the Civilian Conservation Corps in the 1930s.

Otto honored Presidents Washington, Jefferson, Lincoln, McKinley and Wilson by naming monoliths after them.

Most formations bear names that others, following in Otto's bootprints, have bestowed on them.

Upper Monument Canyon has Grand View Spire, Squaw Fingers and Kissing Couple. Lower Monument and Wedding canyons share Praying Hands, Sentinel Spire, Pipe Organ and Mushroom Rock.

Marching along the edge of Rim Rock Drive are Balanced Rock, Saddlehorn and the exotically named Cleopatra's Couch.

Rock climbers have made contributions, including Clueless and Rainbow towers, which cast their shadows in Upper Monument Canyon.

Names serve a purpose, making geological features points of reference. Otherwise, hikers might easily get lost in the canyons. Some names are a century old, while others are fairly recent.

Opposite — Monoliths are the most dramatic feature of Colorado National Monument — sculpted by differing rates of erosion in adjacent layers of hard and soft rock. These intertwined pillars are named Kissing Couple. ■ Photo by Rob Kurtzman

Hank Schoch, the monument's chief park ranger for 17 years, retiring in 1994, memorialized Otto's wedding ceremony at the base of Independence by naming it Wedding Canyon.

Some names have withstood the test of time, while others have disappeared from the lexicon. What Otto called King's Apple Castle became Devils Kitchen.

One of the monument's most distinctive symbols of erosion — a gigantic hole through sandstone overlooking Fruita — lies at the end of a mile-long trail near the visitor center.

Otto named this popular spot Needle's Eye. Today it is Window Rock.

Eric Sandstrom teaches at Mesa State College in Grand Junction and works summers as an interpretive ranger at Colorado National Monument.

■ *Photo provided by National Park Service*

Coke Ovens, seen from the Coke Ovens Overlook. They resemble the old, beehive-shaped ovens used to heat coal for its byproduct coke, which combines with iron ore and limestone to produce iron.

Coke Ovens, 2011. ■ *Photo by Christopher Tomlinson*

With This Ring ...

By Richie Ann Ashcraft

Many couples feel their love has reached monumental heights, which compels them to declare their wedding vows from the top of Colorado National Monument.

In the past 100 years, the sandstone cliffs have witnessed an estimated 3,000 weddings.

The first recorded was that of monument founder John Otto and his bride, Beatrice Farnham, on June 20, 1911. They wed at the base of Independence Monument on a soft carpet of evergreen boughs.

Contemporary couples still choose the monument for its scenic beauty. A bride's white dress in contrast with the tawny hues of sandstone cliffs against an azure sky makes a beautiful backdrop for photographs.

Heath and Jennifer Langevin were married on May 9, 2009. With 120 guests, it was one of the largest weddings to take place on the monument. ■ *Photo by Forever Yours Photography/Michelle Means*

"It was just such a beautiful setting," said Julie Glassman-Hayde, who married her husband, Park Ranger Frank Hayde, on Oct. 11, 2008. They chose the monument because it reflected their lifestyle and gave them "a special place."

Stephanie Poust, who married her husband, Aaron, on May 26, 2007, wore sparkly, white tennis shoes under her dress to make walking on the rocky terrain easier.

Flower girl Fallyn Davis and ring bearer Jackson Pollard take a break on the rocks during the Langevin-Eller wedding. ■ *Photo by Forever Yours Photography/Michelle Means*

The more adventurous have included a supply of rope and carabiners in their plans. David and Wendy Carrott climbed to the top of Independence Monument to say their vows on Nov. 4, 1990. According to an article in the Nov. 5, 1990, edition of The Daily

Sentinel, friends and family of the couple watched the ceremony through binoculars from a distant overlook.

"It can be a quiet to extravagant event," said Jae Dutilly, administrative support assistant who reserves wedding spaces for the park. "To have the opportunity to be a part of it is just so meaningful to us."

Richie Ann Ashcraft is a multitasking mother of three and, as the first mobile journalist for GJSentinel.com, has reported on a plethora of unusual subjects, all while driving with one hand and holding a reporter's notebook with the other.

Jennifer wore white tennis shoes under her dress to make traversing the sandstone easier on her big day. Her shoes were hand-painted by her sister. ■ *Photo by Forever Yours Photography/ Michelle Means*

Emily Berton and Alex Ridderman exchanged wedding vows at Book Cliffs View shelter, overlooking Wedding Canyon, in a lighthearted and casual ceremony in the summer of 2010. ■ *Photo by Christopher Tomlinson*

Otto Meets His Match

By Kathy Jordan

The unlikely union of two fierce independents happened at the base of, fittingly, Independence Monument.

"Trail girl of the Southwest," is how John Otto described his wealthy bride, Beatrice Farnham, a nearly 6-foot-tall, mink-eyed artist and sculptor from Boston who had navigated the Navajo and Pueblo reservations of New Mexico in search of unique Native American art.

Perhaps he saw in her a loyal trail companion — he gave her a pack burro named Foxy for an engagement gift, after all.

Perhaps she saw in him a fellow adventurer, someone who would not curb her spirit.

"Western men like intelligent women," Farnham was quoted at the time. "I mean real women — women who haven't time for foolishness. Western men don't care for Eastern dolls with empty brains."

When Otto, 41, and Farnham, 35, announced their engagement in May 1911, they undoubtedly believed, like many a soon-to-wed couple, they were going to live a long and happy life together.

Instead, their June 20, 1911, marriage was followed by a quick separation and, eventually, divorce.

The day of John Otto and Beatrice Farnham's wedding, The Daily Sentinel printed Otto's explanation for their unlikely nuptials. "I am doing it not because I believe in the modern marriage system, but because I believe in obeying the law of the land, no matter what it is." ∎ *Photo provided by National Park Service*

Despite publicly eschewing social convention, their private wedding was traditional, save the outdoor location, with Farnham in her mother's head-to-toe white satin dress, carrying a bouquet of wildflowers.

On Aug. 21, 1911, a scant two months after their wedding, Beatrice left Grand Junction to make arrangements to close up her estate in the East. She never returned.

"I tried hard to live his way, but I could not live with a man to whom even a cabin was an encumbrance," she reportedly said.

Their divorce was final in February of 1914 and Beatrice married Dallas Benson, a cowboy and ranch manager from Kansas. Alas, that marriage also was short lived.

Kathy Jordan worked for The Daily Sentinel for 32 years and writes a weekly history column for the newspaper.

Springtime sego lilies bloom in Colorado National Monument. Varieties of sego lilies can be found throughout the West. Another common name for the sego lily is mariposa lily, for the Spanish word for butterfly. ■ *Photo by Christopher Tomlinson*

The Long and Winding Road

By Paul Shockley

They were backward at Colorado National Monument.

That is, those behind the wheel in the 1920s.

Drivers in some cases were forced to shift into reverse and back up what was the first automobile road in the monument. It was the product of early automotive engineering; gravity-fed fuel systems wouldn't work on steep hills.

In 1921 the park opened its first roadway, the Trail of the Serpent, which was pegged at the time as the "crookedest road in the world" and complete with some 52 switchbacks. Visitors had to pull their Model T's to the side, allowing faster-moving traffic to pass.

"It was probably one of the most dangerous roads in its early days," said Monument Superintendent Joan Anzelmo.

Auto owners once replenished their car radiators with the help of a natural spring that flowed in the area through the 1950s.

They get around easier now. From visitor traffic to residents commuting to and from homes in nearby Glade Park, some 350,000 people drive across Rim Rock Drive each year, Anzelmo said.

While founder and monument icon John Otto rode a mule or horseback, Anzelmo said they now increasingly come in oversized RVs, chartered buses or on bicycles — roughly 16,000 pedal up annually.

Rim Rock Drive's motorists occasionally make headlines. None more so than a man whose January 2009 botched suicide try ended with his van tumbling into Red Canyon, only to have the van snared and teetering on a rock sitting some 200 feet above the canyon floor. It was the fourth incident in a five-year period in which someone intentionally, or

Early motorists encountered a host of driving challenges on the 52-switchback Trail of the Serpent. The dirt road was more suited to cattle than cars. ■ *Photo provided by National Park Service*

unintentionally, drove off Rim Rock Drive, Anzelmo said.

Danger along Rim Rock Drive has also been the work of Mother Nature. A flood in 1968 washed out a large section of the road for an entire year, while rockfall in 2000 shut down a stretch near the Upper Liberty Cap trailhead for a month.

Paul Shockley reports on Mesa County's criminal justice system for The Daily Sentinel and doesn't spend as much time in Colorado National Monument as he should.

A Colorado State Patrol officer would have had quite a drive to get to the scene of this monument accident. ∎ *Photo provided by National Park Service*

Rim Rock
Drive. ■ *Photo
provided by
National Park
Service*

Theodore Boss' 1937 Oldsmobile, fall 1938. ■ *Photo by Theodore Boss*

Ken Leis and Kathy Hall-Leis cruise Rim Rock Drive in their classic 1961 Corvette. ■ *Photo by Christopher Tomlinson*

Engineer Thomas W. Secrest in 1931 charted the course for Rim Rock Drive. The detailed plan that followed was designed to maximize scenic impact for motorists. To that end, there are 19 scenic overlooks.

■ *Photo provided by The Daily Sentinel Collection/ Museum of Western Colorado*

A would-be suicide plunge into Red Canyon was stopped by a sandstone shelf, leaving the van and its driver dangling above the canyon floor. After the driver was rescued, Rim Rock Drive was closed while a massive crane was brought in to retrieve the van. Employees with the crane company and the National Park Service, along with the Mesa County Technical Search and Rescue Team, chained the vehicle and removed it, to be hauled away on a flat-bed trailer.

■ *Photo by Christopher Tomlinson*

■ *Photo by Gretel Daugherty*

■ *Photo by Christopher Tomlinson*

Rim Rock Drive on the west end in Fruita Canyon. ■ *Photo provided by National Park Service*

Rim Rock Drive climbs, contorts and twists back on itself for nearly 23 miles, roughly from Grand Junction on the east end to Fruita on the west. Measured as the crow flies, however, the distance from one end to the other is only eight miles. Rim Rock Drive in 1993 was listed on the National Register of Historic Places. ■ *Photo by Christopher Tomlinson*

Chapter 4: Art and Culture

The Monument as Canvas

By Sherida Warner

Inside the 32 square miles of rugged Colorado National Monument, artists inhale that rarified air and gape at a true panorama of the American West.

Shadows play against the strata, flitting provocatively among the towering monoliths and deep, red canyons as golden eagles soar on thermals.

Such scenes imbue artists with the desire and courage to replicate this geographical marvel.

Oil painter George Callison of Grand Junction calls the area "an endlessly fascinating wonderland" that's practically in his backyard.

Painting outdoors allows the retired paleontologist to see the play of light and shadow against the true colors of his chosen scene.

Callison determines areas of emphasis, how to mix the appropriate colors and how sharp or soft to make the edges of his shapes. He studies the rock and vegetation patterns.

"Clouds move, sun angle changes, winds blow, gnats bite, fingers stiffen and turn blue with cold," he said of the seasonal challenges.

Yet in the act of painting, Callison becomes entranced.

The entire process is "exhausting, frustrating, yet exhilarating when successful," he said.

For fiber artist Gay Ousley, formerly of Montrose, the rocks in the monument are most captivating, each line well-defined.

"Each portion is revealed as the elements work their relentless magic — ever changing," she said. "And after a rain: vivid."

Ousley, who now lives in Abilene, Texas, continues to create representational pieces of the monument with heightened colors. She uses hand-dyed cottons and silks and densely quilts her layers of fabric.

Sketchbook artist Suzie Garner said her favorite spot is the back porch of the visitor center in the monument. As director of the art department at Mesa State College, she takes students to that area for field sketching workshops.

She finds it particularly challenging to capture the depth of Independence Monument if the sun is high in the sky. Garner has sketched the monolith many times.

"In early morning or afternoon, the light is different and creates values on the rock formations that help an artist get that depth in their drawings," Garner said.

Collage artist Gayle Gerson lives right at the foot of the monument but is reluctant to portray the red rocks. They seem overwhelming to her. Instead, she may depict a lone tree on Serpents Trail, an easy hike not far from her home.

Although she's a native flat-lander, Sherida Warner rarely misses an opportunity to take visiting friends on a tour of the monument. These treks always reinvigorate her imagination as both a writer and fabric artist.

In the spring of 2009, Emma Suzanne Kimball, age 17 at the time, posed at Colorado National Monument. ■ *Photo by Rena M. Kimball*

"Kissing Couple Vista" ■ *Oil painting by John Lintott*

"Serpent's Trail" from Mesa State College Art Collection ■ *Collage panel by Gayle Gerson*

"Snow Fire" ■ *Oil painting by George Callison*

"Winter Shadows" ■ *Oil painting by George Callison*

"Taking in the View" ■ *Art quilt by Bonny Stonemark*

"Evening at Devil's Kitchen" ■ *Oil painting by John Lintott*

"Good Morning Grand Junction"
■ *Oil painting by George Callison*

"Edge of Red Canyon" ■ *Oil painting by John Lintott*

S. GARNER
5.1.2010
VIEW FROM RED CANYON
PULLOUT — COLORADO
NATIONAL MONUMENT

■ *Pen and ink watercolor by Suzie Garner*

"Sierra Vista" ■ *Fiber art by Rita Faussone; photo by Frank Nored*

99

"4th of July" ■ *Oil painting by George Callison*

"Monument Valley" ■ *Fiber art by Gay Ousley; photo by Steve Butman*

Opposite — "Little Park View" ■ *Oil painting by George Callison*

"Dizzying Heights" ■ *Oil painting by George Callison*

"Silent Sentinels" ■ *Fiber art by Susan Strickland; photo by Frank Nored*

English dramatist, author and poet Frank Speaight in March 1938 gave a dramatic reading of Charles Dickens literature to a rapt audience across the flickering footlights of Grand Junction Baptist Church.

The reading was sponsored by The Daily Sentinel as part of a long-standing commitment to support the arts. In a scrapbook, Publisher Walter Walker's secretary, Marion Fletcher, included a poem Speaight penned while visiting the Grand Valley, "inspired by his drive through Monument Canyon and other points of interest in and around Grand Junction."

"Grand Junction of Colorado"

A name too small for such a mighty
*   bowl of awe-inspiring grandeur:*
A world of men should pour into
*   this God-like Valley*
Ringed around with snow-capped hills
*   That touch the moon.*

With God and Time and Space
*   I stood upon a jut of sandstone rock*
And looked into that Nature's scoop
*   of pulsing silences.*
I felt alone with only God for my
*   Companion.*
Oh man how small thou art compared
*   with Ever-lasting Time —*
The Architect of this army of
*   Cathedrals all around me.*
With pigmies seem the Dictators of
*   this age*
Who snarl and bite and quarrel over
*   that which could be buried here —*
Buried here and lost.

Perhaps GRAND JUNCTION you are
*   rightly called —*
For here is Earth with God combined.

■ *Photo by Christopher Tomlinson*

Overleaf — Inspiration literally means "breathed upon." Whether that breath is from deity, muse or inner psyche, many artists find inspiration is more readily accessible in the wide-open expanses of nature.
■ *Photo by Christopher Tomlinson*

Picture This

By Christopher Tomlinson

Within hours of flying into Grand Junction for the first time, at the age of 17, I was in the monument, climbing its red rock walls and making the first of thousands of photos I've shot over the past 35 years.

Those first photos were shot with a 110-cartridge Instamatic camera. I was so taken by the beauty of the monument that I bought a home with a grand view of its east end.

As always, the most dramatic light comes at the first and last light of the day — but there is no bad time to make pictures in the monument. Some of my favorites were taken on a foggy day, in the rain, in the snow and at night. I've often sat on the rim overlooking Independence Monument and watched the fog roll in and out, the sun burning off the mist at first light and seeing the beautiful sunlight paint the canyon walls a fiery red.

You don't need a top-of-the-line camera; an inexpensive digital model or a disposable film camera will work fine. The key is to get out and shoot.

All of the overlooks offer spectacular views, but be sure to get out on one of the trails. The Alcove Nature Trail and Otto's Trail are both short and offer a chance for one-on-one time with the monument, and give you your best chance of making a picture that hasn't been shot a thousand times.

The Liberty Cap and Monument Canyon trails from the bottom are longer, but give the hiker a view from inside the canyon. Also, if you get a chance to fly over the monument, you'll get a much different perspective.

I'm sorry I missed crossing paths with John Otto. He would have made a great hiking buddy. I've climbed Independence Monument, all

Frontier Airlines used this 1970s photo taken at Colorado National Monument for promotions. ■ *Photo provided by Museum of Western Colorado*

450 vertical feet of it, with the help of modern ropes, climbing shoes and a lead climber. Otto climbed it with a lot less support more than 100 years ago. No way!

The Grand Valley is blessed to have one of the most beautiful and accessible tracts of land in the world right here in our backyard. Happy hiking.

Daily Sentinel Chief Photographer Christopher Tomlinson, tree hugger and rock hugger, remembers thinking the first time he hiked in Colorado that it was like coming home to a place he'd never been before.

106

TOMLINSON

Christopher Tomlinson was honored to have his photography of Colorado National Monument featured in the park's centennial year on its visitor passes, visitor guides and in visitor center displays.

A jet plane crosses a half-moon in Monument Canyon.

Pipe Organ casts a long, fog-penetrating shadow into Wedding Canyon.

Opposite — Fog fills the Grand Valley below the monument.

Overleaf — A wide-angle lens captures the panorama of the monument and a polarizing filter helps reproduce the rich colors of the red rock and the deep blue of Western skies. ■ *Photo by Christopher Tomlinson*

DAUGHERTY

When she's not carrying a camera onto the monument on assignment for The Daily Sentinel, Gretel Daugherty loves to share a picnic dinner with her family on a ledge near Cold Shivers Point and watch the sun set across the valley.

Opposite — Although the rock formation in the center doesn't have an official name, many call it the "Titanic" for its resemblance to the bow of a sinking ship.

Light paints the edges of the spires of Monument Canyon.

Right — In this one frame are three diverse geographic regions of the Grand Valley: Colorado National Monument in the foreground, Mount Garfield, back and to the left, and in the back right is Grand Mesa, a spruce-and-aspen-covered flat-top mountain that is over 11,000 feet in elevation and home to Powderhorn Ski Resort.

HUMPHREY

Daily Sentinel photographer Dean Humphrey was inspired as a child to take up photojournalism after a neighbor, Roy Stryker, showed him the work he coordinated for the Farm Security Administration in the 1930s, documenting the Dust Bowl.

Winter snow hushes the high-desert landscape.

Praying Hands, right, and Pipe Organ seemingly hover in the mist.

Opposite —Framed this way, monument topography plays a supporting role to the starring deep-blue sky.

115

KURTZMAN

The challenge of photographing Colorado National Monument is to recapitulate the essence of the monument and its features; the great expanse of some of the canyons with all of their intricate detail, the atmosphere, light, temperature and wind and translate it all into a two-dimensional representation that elicits the same emotion and feelings for the viewer.

I enjoy all aspect ratios but particularly the panorama because it lends itself so well to mimicking our eyes' field of gaze. When panoramic views are combined with near and far visual elements, appropriate exposure, color temperature and optimal light, it all comes together. Regardless of how many times the monument has been photographed or depicted in paintings there is always the opportunity to show it in a new way. It forces the artist to look for new opportunities and different perspectives.

Dr. Rob Kurtzman, a forensic pathologist and former coroner, grew up in New York and Philadelphia, but his favorite place to photograph is the monument.

Opposite – A pinyon pine grabs hold on a rock ledge. When there is enough summer moisture, pinyons produce flavorful pine nuts on which both animals and people feast.

Snow outlines the gnarled fingers of Praying Hands formation.

Overleaf – Erosion resistance of different rock formations is illustrated in Red Canyon, where Red Canyon Creek was able to cut through the softer red Chinle Formation, forming cliffsides, but only notch the Precambrian gneiss of the canyon floor. ■ *Photo by Rob Kurtzman*

117

Precious humidity — the monument receives only some 11 inches of moisture a year — makes for a luxurious, palpable haze in this early-morning shot.

TRAUDT

A true photographic jewel, Colorado National Monument attracts shutterbugs of all skills. For best results, keep in mind the following tips for your next foray into this rich landscape.

• Probably no tip is more important than timing your visit for the "sweet" light: early morning or later in the afternoon. The light is warmer and shadows are longer, giving you shape and dimension.

• Keep an eye on the weather. Dramatic storms regularly roll across the monument, making for spectacular clouds, fog and even lightning.

• When shooting the "big" picture, try to include a foreground object such as a tree, rock or person to give scale and depth. Next tip is related.

• If your camera allows aperture selection, a small aperture (f-stop)

120

Shadows add another implied dimension to this succession of formations.

Observed closely enough, even the rocks are alive. These are covered with lichen — small algae and fungus plants that grow symbiotically.

gives greater depth-of-field for expanded areas of sharp focus.

• A polarizing filter can add drama to skies and clouds while making colors more pure.

• Use a tripod as it slows you down, allows you to fine-tune your composition and produces sharper images. Really!

• Keep the ISO setting low, such as 100 or 200, for smoother, less-grainy photographs.

• Don't just shoot the obvious sweeping vista. Tell the whole story with details of gnarled trees, desert flowers, a lizard or texture on a lichen-covered boulder.

• Take a hike to get off the asphalt. Even a short walk brings you to secret vantage points with surprising visual treats.

• And the best tip of all … buy an annual entrance pass. It supports the monument while encouraging you to make regular visits.

Living in Glade Park for 13 years, photography instructor Steve Traudt traveled through the monument several times per week, but never without his camera.

Overleaf — Sunlight both arrives and recedes in sharp-edged layers over canyon walls. ■ *Photo by Steve Traudt*